BRAVE LADIES

WHO CHANGED THE WORLD
coloring book

A FEMINIST Celebration OF Courageous Women

VOLUME 2

WRITTEN AND ILLUSTRATED BY
KAELEE JENSEN
EDITED BY THE MOST
SUPPORTIVE DAD IN THE WORLD
MICHAEL L. JENSEN

Little
REBEL
ROSIE

Printed in the United States of America

"Understand well as I may, my comprehension can only be an infinitesimal fraction of all I want to understand."

Ada Lovelace

Who was Ada Lovelace?

1815-1852

Ada was an enchantress of numbers.

She was the daughter of the famous poet Lord Byron, though he was completely absent from her life and deserves no credit for her genius. Her mother, Lady Annabella Byron, made sure Ada was educated by the best tutors at a time when most girls weren't allowed a quality education. Lady Byron insisted her daughter be well versed in science and mathematics in hopes that she would be spared the eccentricity and madness of her father. Ada was fascinated by machines and, at age 12, designed a sophisticated flying machine after studying the flight of birds.

A famous mathematician was very impressed by the teenage Lovelace, and remarked that, if she were a boy, she would have a bright future. He worried that women's minds were not meant for such difficult work and warned her that she would fall ill if she continued. She persisted!

Ada first encountered Charles Babbage and his adding machine when she was 17. The inventor and mechanical engineer caught her attention. He, in turn, was impressed by the young girl's intellect, analytical skills, and mathematical ability. Babbage was working on a machine which he called the Difference Engine that would be able to calculate difficult equations flawlessly. Before the Difference Engine was complete, Babbage abandoned it to work on a more advanced machine called the Analytical Engine.

Ada's understanding of the Analytical Engine in some ways surpassed that of Babbage himself. She understood that a machine might someday be programmed to discern symbols as well as numbers. Such a machine would have the capability of calculating not only mathematical equations, but also composing music, creating graphics, and so much more given the right programming and inputs. This was an extraordinary leap for Ada to make and one that many of her male peers struggled to understand. It is no exaggeration to say that she was a century ahead of her time.

As is customary throughout history, when a woman outshines men in their field, many have tried to downplay and discredit Lovelace's contributions to early computing. More recent and in-depth analysis of her correspondence with Babbage proves that she truly was a genius and a visionary of computing.

Audrey Hepburn

"As you grow older, you will discover that you have two hands, one for helping yourself, the other for helping others."

Who was Audrey Hepburn?

1929-1993

Audrey was the epitome of elegance and humility.

She was arguably the most adored actress of all time, but throughout her life she seemed wholly unaware of her beauty, her sophistication, and her fame. Born in Belgium to a Dutch Baroness, she was abandoned by her radicalized Fascist father at age 6, which affected her for the rest of her life. She spent her early years traveling, and could speak five languages. When WWII began, her mother relocated the family to the Netherlands in hopes of avoiding German occupation. However, the Germans did come, and Audrey and her family witnessed and experienced horror and starvation. Audrey's slender stature was the result of malnutrition during wartime hardship. An English sounding name was considered dangerous during the German occupation, so she assumed the more Dutch sounding Edda van Heemstra for safety.

After the war her family moved to Amsterdam where she began formal training in Ballet. She later moved to London to continue her training. Her teacher advised her to abandon Ballet due to the physical toll it was taking on her malnourished body, so she reluctantly decided to focus on acting. She had many minor roles before being cast as the lead in Gigi on Broadway. Soon after she was cast in the starring role in the film Roman Holiday, for which she won an Academy Award and Golden Globe. She went on to star in 21 more films, along with the biggest male co-stars of the golden age, winning many more awards.

Audrey married fellow actor Mel Ferrer and gave birth to her first son Sean. She also suffered several miscarriages during this time. Audrey and Mel eventually divorced, and she married again and gave birth to another son, Luca, and had another miscarriage. After her second divorce she became involved with Dutch actor Robert Wolders and spent what she would call the best years of her life as his companion.

She reunited with her father in the 1960's and despite his lack of affection towards her, she supported him financially until his death. That is just the kind of person Audrey was.

Audrey's Humanitarian work as a UNICEF Ambassador began in the late 1980's. At her appointment as ambassador, she expressed her gratitude for the aid her family had received after enduring the German occupation. She spent the rest of her life traveling the world on UNICEF missions fighting hunger, and working to immunize children. The work was heartbreaking and poignant, but it fulfilled her desire to give back and serve. Everywhere she went, Audrey was well loved by the children, and she loved them. She would pick them up to hold them and hug them regardless of the sometimes deplorable conditions. She said that taking care of children had nothing to do with politics.

Audrey is one of only 12 people who have won Academy, Emmy, Grammy, and Tony Awards. She was awarded the Presidential Medal of Freedom in December 1992 in recognition of her work as a UNICEF Goodwill Ambassador. A month later, Hepburn died of appendiceal cancer at her home in Switzerland at the age of 63.

In 2002 UNICEF honoured Hepburn's legacy of humanitarian work by unveiling a statue, "The Spirit of Audrey", at UNICEF's New York headquarters. Her service for children is also recognised through the U.S. Fund for UNICEF's Audrey Hepburn Society.

"The test for whether or not you can hold a job should not be the arrangement of your chromosomes."

Bella Abzug

Who was Bella Abzug?

1920-1998

Bella persevered.

She grew up poor in the Bronx. From an early age, she was defiant in the face of injustice and decided to become a lawyer. Bella was student body president at tuition free Hunter College, and decided to apply to Harvard Law School, but was rejected due to her gender. She won a scholarship to Columbia University at a time when there were very few female law students across the nation.

She spent her years as a lawyer fighting for Civil Rights, labor and tenants rights, peace, and feminism. She was one of only a few lawyers willing to fight against the unjust Communist witch hunts and prosecutions during the McCarthy era.

Bella helped organize the Women's Strike for Peace in 1961. In order to promote women's issues and to lobby for reform, she helped establish the National Women's Political Caucus with leading feminists Betty Friedan and Gloria Steinem. During this time she was also raising two daughters with her husband Martin. She went on to become an outspoken activist for Gay Rights, and against the war in Vietnam.

Bella won a bid for Congress in 1971 and quickly became a nationally known legislator, one of only 12 women in the House. On her very first day as a Congresswoman, following her conscience, she introduced a bill to withdraw troops from Vietnam. In 1975, Bella made history when she introduced the first Gay Rights bill in Congress. Her many accomplishments in Congress demonstrated her unshakable convictions as an anti-war activist and as a fighter for social and economic justice. She became one of Washington's most colorful and outspoken characters, usually sporting one of her trademark hats. Bella served three terms in Congress before moving on to other causes.

She was appointed by President Carter to co-chair the National Advisory Committee for Women in 1978. She was abruptly fired for criticizing the administration's economic policies in 1979.

Abzug founded and ran several women's advocacy organizations, and continued her work as a lawyer, author, and lecturer. She played a major role at the United Nations, working to empower women around the globe.

She died on March 31, 1998 from complications following heart surgery.
Today the Bella Abzug Leadership Institute is working to maintain her legacy - supporting and training young women to become the leaders of tomorrow.

"Be bold. If you're going to make an error, make a doozy, and don't be afraid to hit the ball."

Billie Jean King

Who is Billie Jean King?

Born: 1943

Billie Jean is a crusader.

Billie Jean was a very athletic child and participated in several sports. At age 11 she bought her own racket and began tennis, practicing daily at the public park. She realized as she looked around that everyone on the tennis courts was white and privileged and she knew it was wrong. "Where is everyone else?" she asked herself. Then and there she decided to become the best tennis player in the world so she could make the sport accessible to everyone.

Billie Jean made her Grand Slam debut at the 1959 U.S. Championships at age 15. She lost in the first round, but over the following decade she became one of the best female tennis players in the world. She was always engaged in a fierce rivalry with world ranked #1 Margaret Court. In 1968, she finally claimed the world's #1 ranking in Women's Tennis herself.

Prize money awarded to female tennis players was usually a fraction of what the male competitors received. In 1970, an outspoken and courageous group of daring young women – Billie Jean King, Rosemary Casals, Judy Tegart Dalton, Nancy Richey, Peaches Bartkowicz, Kristy Pigeon, Valerie Ziegenfuss, Julie Heldman, and Kerry Melville Reid – put their careers at risk in order to put an end to this injustice. This group became known as the "Original 9." Their calls for equal prize money were ignored, so they went against the United States Tennis Association and formed their own tour of eight professional tournaments for women. USTA officials threatened that they would be banned from Grand Slam events. They went ahead anyway. Billie became the first woman to win over $100,000 in one year.

In 1973 the campaign for pay equality gained a worldwide audience of over 90 million when Billie Jean battled tennis player and self-proclaimed chauvinist Bobby Riggs in the "Battle of the Sexes." Bobby had claimed the women's game was inferior to the men's and Billie accepted his challenge to prove him wrong. Prove him wrong she did, winning 6-4, 6-3, 6-3. It was a huge win for Billie Jean, for Women's tennis, and for women in all sports across the country.

Billie Jean and her fellow female players paved the way for the establishment of the Women's Tennis Association (WTA) tour that was formed in 1973. In the same year that the WTA tour was formed, the U.S. Open offered equal prize money to both men and women for the first time.

Married to her devoted husband Larry King since 1965, Billie Jean had realized in the early 70s that she was a lesbian and she started a relationship with a woman named Marilyn. Both Larry and Marilyn were huge supporters of Billie's tennis career, but in 1981 Marilyn sued Billie Jean for support after their relationship ended, forcing her to come out publicly, and as a result, she lost all of her endorsement deals. Since that time she has been a fierce advocate and supporter of LGBT+ rights. She and Larry divorced, and Billie found lasting love with her partner Ilana Kloss. They reside in New York, and remain close friends with Larry and his second wife, and are godparents to his children.

Billie's contributions to tennis are profound. She has formed many tournaments, served on many boards, and started foundations. She has helped tennis become a more equal and accessible sport. She has taught and mentored future generations, including the famous sisters Serena and Venus Williams. In 2009, she was awarded the Presidential Medal of Freedom, the United States' highest civilian honor, by President Obama for her advocacy work on behalf of women and the LGBTQ+ community .

"I just do whatever it is that i believe I should do, regardless of the risks to my life."

Corazon Aquino

Who was Corazon Aquino?

1933-2009

Corazon is the Mother of Filipino Democracy.

She was born into a prominent and politically influential family in the Philippines. Her nickname was Cory. She spent her childhood in the Philippines before her family moved to the United States where she attended high school and college. She decided to return home to pursue a career in law, but that was put on hold when she married her old friend Benigno "Ninoy" Aquino, Jr. and started a family.

Her husband entered politics and was elected Mayor, followed by service as Governor and then Senator. He was known for criticising President Ferdinand Marcos for his power hungry and corrupt regime. Marcos was originally elected in 1965, and re-elected in 1969. In 1972 Marcos declared Martial Law, and sent all political opponents to prison, including Ninoy. Marcos remained in power for the next 14 years, for a total of 21 years, transforming the Phillipines from a Democracy, to a Dictatorship.

Ninoy was imprisoned for 7 years. He continued to oppose Marcos, even from inside prison, and almost died when he went on a 40 day hunger strike. Ninoy had a heart attack while imprisoned and was sent with his family to the U.S. to recuperate in exile. After several years, he returned to the Philippines to challenge the dictatorship of Marcos. His supporters across the country were planning to welcome him home with yellow ribbons. Ninoy was assassinated at the airport on the tarmac as he exited the plane. The public was outraged and yellow became the color of the opposition.

Cory returned to attend his funeral and vowed to continue Ninoy's work in opposing Marcos. She became the unofficial leader of the opposition party in support of returning the Philippines to a Democracy, always wearing her trademark yellow. Though she considered herself to be a "simple housewife", she began leading protests and demonstrations, quickly gaining the support of the people.

In 1985 Marcos decided to hold a snap election due to public discontent, and outside pressure from foreign allies. Cory was hesitant to run for office, but after receiving a petition with over one million signatures she decided to enter the race. Marcos ran a sexist campaign and made sure that he received most of the media coverage. Cory was fearless, and always ready with a witty response to his sexist comments.

He won a rigged election which caused a national uproar. Cory gained the support of prominent people, including some of the military leaders, and she led a protest against him known as the People Power Revolution. Marcos fled the Philippines and Corazon was inaugurated as the first Female President of not only the Philippines, but of any Asian country.

Cory immediately created a Commission charged with drafting a new constitution, and returned the Philippines to Democracy. The new constitution was ratified and Cory implemented many changes, including paying off much of the debt Marcos had accrued during his dictatorship. She was able to restore peace and order. During her presidency she dealt with a volcanic eruption, typhoons, earthquakes, widespread blackouts, and seven coup attempts. She decided to step down after one term as an example to her people that the presidency should have term limits.

When General Fidel Ramos won the 1992 election he praised her saying, "She made our Democracy a fortress against tyrants". Cory's undying faith that Democracy could be won through peaceful dissent proves what a self-proclaimed "simple housewife" can accomplish.
She died from colon cancer in 2009.

In 2010, Cory's son and Ninoy's namesake, was elected President of the Philippines, following in his mother's footsteps. During his campaign he too sported the Aquino family color. Yellow.

Coretta Scott King

"Hate is too great a burden to bear. It injures the hater more than it injures the hated."

Who was Coretta Scott King?

1927-2006

Coretta was known as the mother of the Civil Rights movement.

Coretta was born into an African American family in Marion, Alabama. It was a time when black school children were segregated into one-room schoolhouses, while white children attended larger, better schools. Coretta's parents were determined to provide their children with the best education possible under the circumstances. Her early ambition was music and she became a talented pianist, violinist, and singer. She was appointed as her church's choir director at the young age of 15. She earned degrees in Music and Education from Antioch College, and the New England Conservatory of Music. During her college years she became a very active member of the NAACP. She published an article in Freedom Magazine about the expanded freedom and opportunity that attending college as a black woman afforded her.

She met Martin Luther King, Jr., then a doctoral candidate at Boston University's School of Theology, and they were married in 1954. It was a union that would help change the world. The Kings moved to Montgomery, Alabama where he presided as a pastor.

She worked side by side with her husband as he became a leader of the Civil Rights movement, thrust into the spotlight at the age of 26 when he led the successful Montgomery Bus Boycott. While balancing raising 4 children and supporting her husband, Coretta also established her own distinguished career as an activist. She stated that women were the backbone of the Civil Rights movement and without the contribution of women it would never have become the mass movement that it did.

In 1964 President Johnson signed the Civil Rights Act, prohibiting discrimination of all kinds. That same year Martin Luther King, Jr. was awarded the Nobel Peace Prize for combating racial inequality through nonviolence. Coretta pushed him to speak out publicly against U.S. involvement in Vietnam, and when he was not ready she spoke out herself.

Following her husband's assassination in 1968, Coretta led a march in his stead, and soon after she delivered his planned speech at an anti-war protest in New York's Central Park.

Coretta founded the Martin Luther King, Jr. Center for Nonviolent Social Change, and later successfully lobbied for his birthday to be recognized as a Federal holiday. She continued her activism throughout her life, protesting apartheid in Africa, speaking out about Civil Rights, women's and children's rights, poverty, religious freedom, healthcare, and the rights of Gays and Lesbians.

Who was Eleanor Roosevelt?

1884-1962

Eleanor was the dearest kind of friend and a cutthroat opponent.

Born into New York high society, the shy young Eleanor always felt that she was a disappointment to her mother, but was doted on by her father Elliot. He called her Nell and she loved him dearly. Eleanor's childhood took a sad turn when she was orphaned by age 10. She and her siblings then went to live with their grandmother. Eleanor was sent to a progressive boarding school in England as a teenager, a place that helped form the outspoken woman she would become. She was encouraged to be independent and think critically and for the first time in her life she felt a fierce sense of belonging.

She returned to New York and began volunteer work in the lower East Side slums helping young immigrants and the poor. She joined the NY Consumers League which exposed deplorable working conditions for women and children. She met and began dating Franklin D. Roosevelt, and brought him along to the poorer parts of New York, opening his eyes to suffering. He and Eleanor married in 1905 and before long, she was juggling the responsibilities of raising children, running multiple homes, and hosting political gatherings. She joined the League of Women Voters, and the Women's City Club, finding again a community of independent women where she felt she belonged. She was adept at public speaking and consistently surprised crowds and politicians with her wisdom and wit.

Despite knowledge of her husband's infidelities, Eleanor steadfastly supported him after he contracted polio and had a leading role in shaping his political career. Often traveling as his surrogate campaigner in the 1932 Presidential election, she helped him win with the widest margin in history, in large part due to her political knowledge, and her rapport with the lower class in post-Depression America.

During the campaign, she had befriended Lorena Hickok, a female reporter for the Associated Press. "Hick" was assigned to cover Eleanor exclusively and they became very close. The letters they exchanged reveal a very affectionate, intimate, and even romantic relationship between the two women that would last many decades.

Eleanor considered it her duty to be the progressive voice in the President's ear. She vocally promoted equal treatment for women and for African Americans. She worked to get many women appointed to governmental positions and held women-only press conferences, which forced newspapers to hire female reporters. She fought for equal pay legislation, for Civil Rights, and fought against child labor. When the Daughters of the American Revolution refused to allow popular African-American singer Marian Anderson to perform in their Constitution Hall, Eleanor resigned her membership and organized a concert at the Lincoln Memorial instead. She wrote a daily news column for 30 years. She raised money, lobbied Congress, and held her own press conferences on the issues she was passionate about.

During the war she encouraged women to take factory jobs, warned against anti-Japanese attitudes after Pearl Harbor and privately opposed the executive order to send Japanese-Americans to internment camps. She also lobbied her husband to allow greater immigration of groups persecuted by the Nazis, including Jews. However, she was only able to secure political refugee status for eighty-three Jewish refugees.

After her husband's death Eleanor was appointed to the UN by President Truman, where she played an instrumental role in drafting the Universal Declaration of Human Rights.

Eleanor Roosevelt was a woman ahead of her time, and an outspoken advocate for those less fortunate. She ignored arbitrary social rules, and was fierce in her commitment to always do right. The achievements of this great woman are as incalculable as the number of lives she influenced.

"Feet, what do I need you for when I have wings to fly?"

Frida Kahlo

Who was Frida Kahlo?

1907-1954

Frida was defiant.

She was born Magdalena Carmen Frida Kahlo y Calderón in Mexico in 1907. A fierce Mexican patriot, Frida would claim her birth-year was 1910 because that was the year the Mexican Revolution started. "A daughter of the revolution!" she proclaimed. Frida grew up in their family home, La Casa de Azul – The Blue House. Her father was a painter and photographer who introduced Frida to the arts, and encouraged her eccentricities. Frida credited him for making her childhood marvelous. He taught her about literature, nature, and philosophy. He encouraged her to play sports to regain her strength after contracting polio, despite the fact that most physical exercise was seen as unsuitable for girls.

She wore men's suits as a teen, was outrageously witty, and fell in with a group of politically active, intellectual, edgy friends. Frida lived life to the fullest, until a horrific bus accident at the age of 18 left her body mangled and broken. Her dream of attending medical school was crushed. She was bedridden for months, and dealt with the injuries for the rest of her life. During her convalescence, she returned to a childhood hobby of painting. Many of her paintings throughout her life reflect the pain and trauma she experienced as a result of her bus accident.

Frida began wearing traditional Tehuana outfits – clothing of women from a historically matriarchal society which had come to represent an authentic and indigenous cultural heritage. She wore long and colorful skirts, elaborate headdresses and masses of jewelry. Frida considered this to be an expression of her feminist and anti-colonialist ideals.

Frida married famous Mexican artist and Communist activist Diego Rivera, but their marriage was contentious. They were both passionate and dramatic artists and they fought. She would say that she had two major accidents in her life. One was the bus – the other Diego. Diego was unfaithful from the very beginning, leading Frida to have romantic relationships with both men and women outside of her marriage. She had several failed pregnancies, some ending in miscarriage, others in medically necessary abortions. Frida's pelvis was terribly damaged in the bus crash and because of this, she could never have children.

At the beginning of their marriage, Diego was the famous artist, and Frida was known simply as Diego's wife. They traveled the US while Diego painted large murals in various cities. Soon people began to notice Frida's talent as well. Frida painted self-portraits which often depicted an intense morbidity, sadness, and the brokenness of her body. After a successful show in New York, she was invited to Paris, where she famously engaged in a relationship with Josephine Baker. Paris loved Frida, but Frida did not love Paris. Surrealism was the fascination of the day, but Frida did not consider herself as such, saying, "They thought I was a Surrealist, but I wasn't. I never painted dreams. I painted my own reality." While in Paris, Frida became the first 20th century Mexican artist to have a painting displayed in the Louvre.

Frida and Diego were divorced for a short time, but eventually reconciled and remarried. The marriage this time was not as contentious, but they still continued living largely separate lives. They moved back to La Casa De Azul where Frida grew up. Frida became a beloved art teacher, encouraging her students to appreciate Mexican popular culture and folk art. As her health declined over the next decade, she endured many medical procedures, lost a leg, and became addicted to painkillers and alcohol. Her art reflects the pain and disappointment of a broken body, failed medical procedures, and her personal suffering.

Frida gained attention around the world for her art, but not at home in Mexico. Finally, in 1953 she was invited to have an exhibition in her home country. Frida was terribly ill that night, but she refused to miss the event. She had her four-poster bed sent to the gallery, and was driven there in an ambulance. It was a wonderful celebration. Not long after, she died at age 47 at Casa De Azul. Frida was a scarcely known Mexican artist for most of her life and for decades after her death. She has recently been discovered anew, and has grown in popularity worldwide. She has become a Feminist icon, and is an inspiration as a radical artist, political activist, writer, thinker, lover, and disabled bisexual Woman of Color who turned her grief and pain into vibrant and unforgettable art.

"When somebody tells me I cannot do something, that's when I do it."

Gertrude Ederle

Who was Gertrude Ederle?

1905-2003

It's the Roaring Twenties and an unknown swimmer takes the world by storm.

Gertrude grew up in a working-class family in New York City. Nick-named Trudy, she spent her summers swimming in the Atlantic Ocean at their seaside cottage in New Jersey, taking her first strokes as a toddler. She suffered a bout of measles as a child, leaving her partially deaf. Doctors warned that too much swimming might damage her hearing further, but Trudy wouldn't stay dry. As a teen, her sister Margaret pushed her to compete, filling out forms and entering her in competitions while Trudy just wanted to swim. She trained at the Women's Swimming Association facility in Manhattan and began winning events and setting records.

At the 1924 Olympics in Paris, Trudy won a Gold medal and two Bronze medals, setting a world record time in a relay race with her team. By 1925, she had 29 World and U.S. records. Then she undertook the athletic challenge of her life - swimming across the English Channel. Her first attempt ended after nine hours when her trainer, fearing she was in trouble, reached out from the boat to grab her. Under the rules of distance swimming, no member of her team was allowed to touch her while in the water.

Determined to try again, Trudy returned to France in August of 1926. Only five others had ever completed the swim - all men - and there was tremendous bias against female athletes. The media was intrigued by her daring, but people were sure that women simply did not possess the physical strength for such a challenge. On August 6, she put on an outfit designed by her sister to prevent drag in the water. The outfit consisted of a red bathing cap, a scandalous two-piece silk bathing suit and goggles. Slathering herself with lanolin, petroleum jelly, olive oil and lard to protect against jellyfish and cold, she waded into the 61-degree water just after 7:00 a.m. on a beach in France. She gave firm instructions that she was not to be pulled out of the water unless she directly asked to be.

The water was choppy and the currents against her. She swam and swam and swam. Every man who had accomplished the swim had used the breast stroke, but Trudy had been practicing a new stroke called the crawl. Two tugboats accompanied her. Her father, sister, coach and friends were aboard the first, the second boat was occupied by journalists. The spectators began to lose sight of Trudy as the waves rose around their boats and they hollered at her to stop, to give up. She looked up and called, "What for?" She was happy in the frigid water, and pressed on. The 21 mile swim was estimated to have stretched to 35, the bad weather causing Trudy to veer off course. A large crowd had gathered on the English shore, holding flares to light the way. As they spotted her red swimming cap nearing the shore, they cheered her on. Her toes touched the English sand - and in less time than any other swimmer. Her success was announced around the world. The first woman and the sixth person to swim across the English Channel - the fastest of them all! Her time for the Channel crossing was 14 hours 31 minutes, beating the men's record by nearly two hours and remaining the women's record for 35 years.

She was welcomed home to New York City with a ticker tape parade attended by millions. The Mayor of New York City said no homecoming rivaled that of Gertrude Ederle, before or after. President Coolidge invited her to the White House calling her "America's best girl". She traveled the U.S. in a Vaudeville act, portrayed herself in a short film, and was bombarded with marriage proposals. Trudy wasn't made for public life, and she went on to live a relatively quiet existence in a New York apartment. Her name was nearly forgotten as the years went on, which didn't bother her. She swam because she enjoyed it, not for fame. She conquered the Channel simply because she knew she could. Her hearing loss was worsened by the Channel swim and declined more and more over the years. In 1933 she suffered a severe spinal injury when she fell down the stairs of her apartment building. She proved doctors wrong who said she would not swim or walk again, and she appeared in a swimming show at the New York's World's Fair in 1939.

Trudy spent her later years teaching hearing-impaired children to swim. Trudy changed what the world thought of women and their athletic abilities. She proved that the "Fairer sex" was indeed as capable, as athletic, and as able to perform on the same level as men in sports. She died in 2003 at the age of 98.

Who was Junko Tabei?

1939-2016

"There was never a question in my mind that I wanted to climb that mountain, no matter what other people said."

Junko Tabei

Junko Tabei was the first woman to reach the summit of Mount Everest and the first woman to conquer the Seven Summits, climbing the highest peak on every continent.

Growing up in Japan, she was considered a frail, weak child, but fell in love with mountain climbing at the age of 10 when she went on a school climbing trip to Mount Nasu. Although she had a great desire to continue climbing, her family did not have enough money for such an expensive hobby and Junko made only a few climbs during her high school years.

From 1958 to 1962, she studied English Literature and Education at Showa Women's University, in Tokyo, where she was a member of the Mountain Climbing Club. After graduating she joined several climbing groups. She was often the only woman in the group, and some men would refuse to climb with her. Junko kept on exploring Japan's peaks while working long hours as editor of a scientific journal and occasionally tutoring piano and English to pay for her expensive hobby. By the mid-sixties, she had scaled all of Japan's highest mountains, including Mount Fuji.

She met her husband during a dangerous ascent of Mount Tanigawa. He shared her passion for climbing and supported her when, years later, she decided to give up work in order to focus on climbing. The couple had two children; a daughter, Noriko, and a son, Shinya. Leaving her children at home with her husband to go on climbing expeditions was unheard of in Japan where women were still only thought of as homemakers. After facing so much sexism from male climbers, she founded the Ladies Climbing Club with the idea that women could and ought to lead their own expeditions anywhere in the world. She led the club on an expedition to Annapurna III, succesfully summitting in May 1970. Then they set their sights on Mount Everest.

They struggled to find sponsors for the expedition and were frequently told that the women "should be raising children instead." They were given small sums from a local newspaper and a TV station, however all of the group members still had to pay an amount that was almost equal to Japan's average yearly salary. To save money they recycled material from car seats to sew their own waterproof pouches and over-gloves. They also purchased goose feather from China and made their own sleeping bags. Students of the club members even saved Jam packets from their school lunches to add to the supplies.

They began the expedition in the spring of 1975 traveling first to Kathmandu. In early May, while the group was at Camp II at 21,326 feet on Mount Everest, an avalanche struck. The women and their guides were buried under the snow. Junko lost consciousness for approximately six minutes until her Sherpa guide dug her out. Junko's injuries left her unable to walk for the next two days. Determined to finish, she pressed on, summiting Everest 12 days after the avalanche. She was the only woman in her party to summit and she made it, literally on hands and knees. She was showered with attention and praise. She received messages from the King of Nepal, the Japanese government, and many others. A TV miniseries was made about the expedition and she toured Japan making personal appearances. Success brought fame with which she was uncomfortable, but she endured the fame and continued in her love of climbing.

Junko continued in her attempt to conquer the Seven Summits, climbing Kilimanjaro in Tanzania in 1980, Mt. Aconcagua in Argentina in 1987, Denali in Alaska in 1988, Mt. Elbrus in Russia in 1989, and Vinson Massif in Antarctica in 1991, and she completed the Seven Summits in 1992 with her ascent of Jaya Peak in Indonesia. In addition, she set a goal to reach the top of the highest mountain in each country, and she conquered 70 of the peaks on that list.

She later became an environmental advocate and completed graduate studies at Kyushu University, studying the impact of the garbage left on mountains by climbers. She served as director of Himalayan Adventure Trust of Japan, an organization working at a global level to preserve mountain environments. One of her projects as director was to build an incinerator to burn climbers' rubbish. She also led and participated in "clean-up" climbs in Japan and the Himalayas.

Junko was diagnosed with cancer in 2012. Undaunted she continued with many of her mountaineering activities until she died in a hospital in Kawago in 2016.

"I believe dreams help light our darkness and give us the push we need to move across the rink of life."

Kristi Yamaguchi

Who is Kristi Yamaguchi?

Born: 1971

Kristi Yamaguchi is a champion.

She grew up in a Japanese American family in California. Her paternal grandparents and maternal great-grandparents emigrated to the United States from Japan. During World War II Japanese Americans were suspected of disloyalty to America and seen as potential spies and saboteurs. Their homes were seized and businesses closed, and they were sent to internment camps by the thousands. Her grandparents were among those sent to the internment camps, and her mother was born there. Her father also spent part of his young life in an internment camp. It is a shameful part of modern American history, but despite the internment, many Japanese Americans still fought in the war. Her paternal grandfather was in the U.S. Army and fought in Germany and France during World War II. Kristi considers herself and her success a result of the generations of struggle and hardship that her ancestors endured.

Kristi was born with disfigured feet, and spent her earliest years in casts and braces. She took dance as physical therapy to help strengthen her healing feet, and began ice skating at age 6. Kristi looked up to Dorothy Hamill, a Gold Medal-winning Olympic figure skater, and was inspired to work hard and become a champion.

She went on to Capture Gold in both Ladies' singles and pairs at the 1988 World Junior Championships. She skated pairs with Rudy Galindo until 1991, the year she was first crowned World Professional Figure Skating Champion. Kristi skated at the 1992 Winter Olympic games in Albertville, France, where her dreams came true when she won the Olympic Gold! She decided not to compete in another Olympics, and instead traveled the world as a professional figure skater.

Kristi is married to NHL hockey player Bret Hedican, who she met at the 1992 Olympics. They have two daughters and live in California. Kristi is an author, philanthropist, and founder of the Always Dream Foundation, which supports the hopes and dreams of children, and focuses on early childhood literacy.

She recently won Season 6 of ABC's Dancing With the Stars with partner Mark Ballas, and worked with NBC as a special correspondent for the 2010 Winter Olympics in Vancouver and the 2014 Winter Olympics in Sochi, Russia. Kristi has been inducted into the World Skating Hall of Fame and the U.S. Olympic Hall of Fame.

Who is Mae Jemison?

Born: 1956

Mae had big dreams.

While growing up in Chicago, Mae's parents encouraged her in everything she pursued. She was an accomplished dancer, and a curious, and motivated youngster. At a very young age she planned to become a scientist. People told her this was uncommon for a woman, and encouraged her to consider a more acceptable career, but Mae knew better. She refused to allow other people's limited imagination to stop her from following her dreams.

Mae was fascinated by the stars and very knowledgeable about NASA and the Apollo space missions. She was frustrated about the absence of women and people of color in the space program, but was inspired by African American actress Nichelle Nichols' portrayal of officer Nyota Uhura in Star Trek. Mae knew that she could, and would travel into space someday. She was known to spend countless hours in the library studying science.

She graduated from high school at age 16, then attended Stanford with a double major in chemical engineering, and African and Afro-American studies, while studying dance in her free time. At this point she knew she had to decide between becoming a doctor or pursuing dance as a career. She chose to go to medical school. Mae traveled the world to study and practice medicine, studying in Cuba, Kenya, and at a Cambodian refugee camp in Thailand. She went on to earn a PhD in Medicine from Cornell University.

She traveled to Africa and worked as a doctor and as the Peace Corps medical officer for Liberia and Sierra Leone when only 27 years old. She returned to the U.S. to work as a General Practitioner while taking graduate level engineering classes. She had not forgotten her dream of traveling into space. In 1985 she applied to become an astronaut and was selected to train at NASA. She made history in 1992 as the first African American woman in space. She had finally reached the stars! She was a Science Mission Specialist aboard the space shuttle Endeavor, spending 8 days in space conducting scientific experiments. She said that as she flew into space, she looked down at Earth to see her hometown of Chicago and remembered herself as a little girl who loved space, imagining that very moment. Mae brought some interesting objects with her into space - a poster from the dance studio where she studied, and several small art objects from West African countries to symbolize that space belongs to all nations. She also brought a photo of Bessie Coleman - the very first African American woman to fly an airplane

After that mission she retired from NASA and became an environmental studies professor at Dartmouth, started an educational non-profit, an international science camp, and an agency called 100-Year Starship - an initiative working to travel beyond our solar system in the next 100 years.

Mae never planned to be the poster child for African American astronauts, but she realized that her representation matters. She remembered her disappointment in the lack of representation in the fields she wanted to go into as a young person. Her visibility as a Woman of Color in science, medicine, and engineering is important in inspiring future generations to pursue careers in those fields. She is a proponent of integrating science and the arts in education. She believes that the creativity children are taught when participating in the arts is needed for real advancements in science, and imagination must be encouraged for scientists to dream the impossible. She continues to encourage diversity and creativity in STEM today through education and public speaking.

"Each individual brings something different to the same role."

Maria Tallchief

Who was Maria Tallchief?

1925-2013

Maria was a Firebird.

She was born Elizabeth Marie Tall Chief in Oklahoma on the Osage Indian Reservation in 1925. Her mother, Ruth Porter, was a Scots-Irish woman who loved music and dance. Her father, Alexander Tall Chief was an Osage Indian who had become wealthy from oil discovered on the Osage land. She and her sister began training in dance and piano as young as three. Her Grandmother Eliza Big Heart frequently took young Maria and her sister, Marjorie, to the ceremonial tribal dances to expose them to the traditions and customs of the Osage people.

As they grew, their parents became more committed to their daughters' study of the arts and they moved the family to Los Angeles for more formal training when Maria was eight. Maria eventually chose Ballet over piano and trained with esteemed Ballet instructors. She worked and practiced hard throughout her teen years and after high school she moved to New York where she joined the Ballet Russe de Monte Carlo.

There was fierce competition between American and Russian Ballerinas and it was suggested that Maria change her name to something more Russian sounding. Still known as Elizabeth Marie Tall Chief, she was very proud of her Native American heritage. She refused a Russian sounding name, but conceded that there were many Maries and Elizabeths in the world of Ballet. She chose the name Maria and simplified her last name to Tallchief.

Maria became the muse of the revered choreographer George Balanchine, who created many roles specifically for her. They were married in 1946 and spent the next few years together at Ballet Russe. Later, they lived in Paris working for the Paris Opera, then returned to New York where Balanchine founded his own New York City Ballet. He most famously choreographed the role of Stravinsky's Firebird for Maria. At the New York City Ballet, she became recognized as one of the greatest dancers in the world. She became the Prima (lead) Ballerina for the company and held that position for eighteen years. The fact that the first American Prima Ballerina was in fact Native American at a time when Ballet was dominated by Russians and Europeans was remarkable.

With each new company she joined, Tallchief's heritage was greeted with skepticism - she was not the Russian or European Ballerina that people expected. Each time, she had to prove herself, but it did not take long for her talent, dedication, and artistic ability to win out. The public loved Maria Tallchief. Maria was called upon to dance as many as eight performances each week, and her legend grew. She and Balanchine eventually divorced, but continued working together. Maria married again and took some time off to give birth to a daughter, Elise.

She retired from the stage in 1965, and became a ballet teacher in Chicago, where she founded the Ballet School of the Lyric Opera and served as artistic director of the Chicago City Ballet. Maria died in 1993 at the age of 88. In 1996 she was inducted into the National Women's Hall of Fame, and in that same year received a Kennedy Center Honor.

Who was Marsha P. Johnson?

1945-1992

Marsha was unapologetically herself.

Marsha was assigned male at birth, named Malcolm Michaels, Jr. and grew up in New Jersey. She was around 5 when she began to wear dresses, but felt pressure to stop because of other children's aggression. She graduated from high school and moved to New York City with $15 and a bag of clothes. Sometimes she was Malcolm. Sometimes she was Marsha. She identified as a drag queen, and transvestite*. When asked what the P stood for she responded, "for Pay it no mind".
A phrase she used often.

It was a time when almost everything Marsha considered herself to be was criminalized. Marsha was often arrested, and stopped counting after the number hit 100. In 1969 Marsha was at the Stonewall Inn, a local hangout for outliers in the LGBTQ+ community. The police stormed in and started arresting people for crossdressing. As the story goes, a scuffle broke out between police and a Drag King named Storme Delarverie. Storme yelled at the surrounding crowd to do something, and may have thrown a punch at the cop. Marsha liked to say that she herself threw a shot glass which really started the whole thing. Marsha called it "The shot glass heard round the world". Fighting broke out which sparked an uprising against the police around the city. This rebellion lasted several days and gained national attention. It has been called a riot, others claim it was an act of civil disobedience. They were sick and tired of unfair treatment by the police for simply being themselves. Their bravery, along with that of others at the bar that night, led to the Gay Liberation movement. One year after the riots the first Gay Pride Parades were held, and two years after, there were Gay Rights groups in every major American city.

Marsha became a flamboyant fixture of street life in Greenwich Village. Andy Warhol featured her in an art show about Transgender Men and Women. She was called the Saint of Christopher Street, and the Queen of the Christopher Piers. She wore extravagant dresses adorned in glitter and puffed sleeves, with flowers and fake fruit decorating her hair. She was known for her kindness and generosity, in spite of the hard life she was living. When she begged for money or food, she turned right around and shared it with others in need. She often slept on the streets for long periods between living arrangements, and she suffered several mental breakdowns. Sometimes taunted and heckled for her appearance, she kept on with a smile on her face. "Pay it no mind" she would say as she walked on by.

Marsha and her friend Sylvia Rivera founded STAR - Street Transvestite* Action Revolutionaries - a group dedicated to helping homeless young drag queens and trans women of color. They dedicated their lives to the fight for equality for the LGBTQ+ community, but they themselves never benefited much from the fight. They were frequently disparaged and left behind by the white Gay men who considered them a hindrance to further progress and acceptance for Gay Rights. Marsha didn't want acceptance, she did not want to blend in - Marsha demanded liberation for all! She spent much of her time at the bedside of beloved friends as the Gay community suffered and lost to the AIDS epidemic. She herself was diagnosed with the disease too.

Marsha's body was found in the Hudson River in 1992. The police ruled her death a suicide, but those who knew her believe her death was suspicious and suspect she was murdered.

*at the time of the Stonewall riots, the gay community did not have the same extensive vocabulary to describe sexuality as we do today. Marsha and Sylvia were transgender women, but primarily referred to themselves as drag queens or transvestites, which have separate meanings today. Transvestite is now considered a derogatory term

Who was Martha Hughes Cannon?

1857-1932

Martha Hughes Cannon

She was a physician, the first female State Senator in the United States, an advocate, suffragette and a sister wife. Martha Hughes Cannon was a remarkable, complicated woman.

Nicknamed Mattie, she grew up as a Mormon in the territory of Utah. Though the rest of the country considered Mormon women oppressed due to the practice of polygamy, women in Utah actually had more rights than most - the right to own land, to vote, to establish businesses, and to divorce their husbands. LDS church leader Brigham Young encouraged women to learn and work to help support their families.

Mattie became a typesetter for the local newspaper as a teen, and later for the influential paper, the Women's Exponent. She worked as a school teacher while attending the University of Deseret. She defiantly cut her hair short, caring for it was too much of a burden. She graduated with a degree in Chemistry in 1875 and boarded a train to attend medical school at the University of Michigan, which had just begun admitting women, though they could not attend in the same classrooms as men. Mattie, and the few other women who were enrolled, attended women-only courses. In her free time she took night classes to study bacteriology.

Mattie graduated as a doctor of medicine and then became the first female student at the University of Pennsylvania Auxiliary Medical Department, while also attending the National School of Elocution and Oratory to study public speaking, lecturing, drama, and performance.

She returned to Utah in 1882 at age 25, began a private practice and was called to be the resident physician at the new Deseret Hospital, founded by women. She decided to marry an older man who sat on the board of the Deseret Hospital. His name was Angus Munn Cannon.

Angus already had 3 wives when he married her. Mattie believed fiercely that polygamy was ordained by God, but it was a decision that would derail her promising future. The government was cracking down on the practice of polygamy in Utah, so they married in secret.

Her husband was soon prosecuted for living illegally with his other plural wives and was fined and sentenced to 6 months in prison. She fled to rural Utah to give birth to their daughter and keep their marriage a secret.

Physicians who attended births of polygamous families were being forced to testify against their patients, and Mattie refused to do so. She exiled herself in refusal to cooperate, fleeing to England with their daughter. She returned after two years, reestablished her practice, and founded a nursing school - only to flee again at the birth of her second child. Mattie never received the support and help she deserved and expected from her husband, who was busy with his other wives and children. She struggled financially and lived as a single mother for her whole life.

In 1890, under pressure from federal officials, LDS Church President Wilford Woodruff advised members of the church to "follow the law of the land". This devastated the polygamous families, who considered their marriages Holy. However, this meant with the appearance of cooperation by the Mormon community, prosecutions would end. It also meant the promise of Statehood in Utah.

Utah had approved suffrage in 1870, but the Federal government revoked that in 1887. With statehood on the horizon, women mobilized and agitated to regain their right to vote. Mattie quickly became a leader in the Utah Woman's Suffrage Association, giving talks to groups throughout Utah and participating in suffrage conferences in the East along with Susan B. Anthony and Elizabeth Cady Stanton. She traveled to Chicago with a group of Utah women leaders to the 1893 Columbia Exposition, where Mattie was a featured speaker at the Women's Congress. She went on from Chicago to appear before a congressional committee in Washington, D.C., to give a status report on the women's suffrage work in Utah. People were surprised by the contradiction of an "oppressed polygamous woman" who was well educated, well spoken, and traveled independently to speak publicly.

When Utah became a state in 1896, women had won the right to vote, as well as run for office. Martha ran for State Senator as a Democrat. Among the other candidates was her husband Angus, who ran as a Republican. Press across the nation enjoyed the prospect of a husband and wife running against each other in different political parties. When the results were in, Martha Hughes Cannon became the first woman elected to a State Senate in U.S. history. It would be 25 more years before the rest of the nation's women would join her in the right to vote.

Senator Cannon dove into her passions for health and service, introducing bills to provide education for disabled children, and protecting the health of women and children, and female employees. She created the state's first Board of Health. Her study of bacteriology made her a tireless advocate for sewers and public sanitation. She eventually spoke on suffrage to the U.S. House Committee on the Judiciary. Mattie gave a long and elegant address describing the positive effects of women having the right to vote in her state. She was invited to a reception at the White House where she met President McKinley.

During her second term Mattie became pregnant for a third time, proving that the Mormons were not following the manifesto against polygamy. She stayed in office through the birth, but the scandal prevented her from furthering her political career. She spent the rest of her life practicing medicine, raising children and grandchildren, and serving the poor. After the death of her husband, she settled in California.

Mattie was a humble woman of faith who made national history. She played an important role in pursuing equal rights, and she vastly improved the health and lives of thousands, all while struggling to support herself and her children financially. Mattie met men on their own ground and won, and she did it 130 years ago. The Utah State Department of Health building is named in her honor, and in 2018 the Utah State Legislature voted to place her statue in Statuary Hall in the Capitol building in Washington, DC in 2020.

"Every-thing I do is for my people."

Sacagawea

Who was Sacagawea?

1788-1812 (?)

Sacagawea was a survivor.

Sacagawea's story is a complex and sad one. She herself was already a victim of childhood kidnapping, enslavement, and stolen girlhood when she was brought along on the famous Lewis and Clark expedition.

She was an ordinary Shoshone girl living with her tribe near the Salmon river in what is now Idaho. An enemy tribe kidnapped Sacagawea and several other young girls during a battle, and took them to their native North Dakota. The Hidatsa tribe then sold her and perhaps one other girl to a French Canadian fur trapper named Toussaint Charbonneau. History writes that Sacagawea became his wife, but at the time she had already been kidnapped, sold, and was very young, so the nature of the "marriage" is disputed. She was soon pregnant with a son. It was at this time that Lewis and Clark's Corps of Discovery enocuntered Charbonneau who had with him two young Shoshone "wives". Unlike anyone else in the expedition, Charbonneau spoke passable Hidatsa, and Sacagawea spoke Shoshone and Hidatsa. This was valuable to the expedition, and despite Sacagawea's pregnancy, she and Charbonneau were hired. Sacagawea gave birth to a healthy baby boy Jean-Baptiste in the early spring of 1805. Fifty-five days later, when the snow had melted Sacagawea was famously strapping the infant on her back for the long walk to Oregon with the Corps of Discovery.

She turned out to be a valuable addition to their team. Just a few months into the journey, one of the canoes capsized, spilling all of it's contents into the river. Sacagawea dove in the water to single handedly retrieve the valuable documents and critical supplies. Lewis wrote of his gratitude toward "the Indian woman". Months later, around Three Forks, Montana, the Corps bumped into Sacagawea's own tribe who she hadn't seen since her kidnapping. Her brother was now Chief of the tribe and she bubbled with joy at the reunion with him and her people. Her role as interpreter was a tricky one. The Tribal Elders spoke to her in Shoshone. She relayed their words in Hidatsa to Charbonneau, who spoke in French to a Corps member. He then translated that into English. They negotiated trades for horses and enlisted the Shoshone to help shepherd the group safely across the Rocky Mountains. At one point the Corps had been surviving by eating tallow candles and Sacagawea foraged and dug for Camas roots, cooking food nutritious enough to nurse them back to health. She earned great respect from the explorers and was included in planning routes and voting during big decisions.

When they arrived near the Oregon coast they heard stories of a massive beached whale on the shore and a small party from the Corps decided to venture to the beach. At first Sacagawea was not included in this party but she made a pretty big deal out of seeing both the ocean and the whale, and went along. By the time they were on their way home, Sacagawea's infant son had turned one year old. Clark had become fond of the boy, and nicknamed him "Pompy". They soon arrived back in North Dakota, and the members said goodbye to Charbonneau, Sacagawea, and Jean-Baptiste. The family then returned to Hidatsa country. For his services to the mission as interpreter, Charbonneau was paid around $500, Sacagawea received nothing.

Clark later wrote to Charbonneau offering to help the family settle in St. Louis, where he would guarantee their son an education. After some years spent among the Hidatsa tribe, Sacagawea, Charbonneau, and their son moved to Missouri where Jean-Baptiste studied in St. Louis, and his parents lived at a nearby fort.

At this point history gets fuzzy. Some believe Sacagawea died of fever leaving behind an infant daughter. Others believe she lived a long life after reuniting with the Shoshone in the Wind River Range. There is just enough evidence to support both theories, but prove neither.

Sacagawea's name is well-known, though the true story of her life remains a mystery. There are more statues celebrating her across the U.S. than any other woman. She is an American icon, despite the fact that we really don't know much about her. What we do know is that the celebrated and peaceful Lewis and Clark expedition for which she served as interpreter, was just the beginning of the U.S. government's shameful assault on Native lands, and eventual genocide of Native people and culture.

Who was Shirley Chisholm?

1924-2005

Shirley had guts.

She was born in Brooklyn to working class immigrant parents who sacrificed to provide their children with a good education. They lived in Barbados for part of her childhood where she credited the strict, traditional, British-style schools for giving her a good start. The family then moved back to Brooklyn where she attended a highly regarded girl's high school. To qualify for a city college you had to have good grades, and considering the poverty in black neighborhoods, few black students were able to meet those requirements. They just weren't given the same resources and opportunities as white students. Shirley worked hard and was admitted to Brooklyn college on a free tuition program as one of a few minority students. She won awards on the debate team and her professors encouraged her to consider a political career, but she felt she faced a "double handicap" as both black and female, and wasn't optimistic about the idea.

Initially, Shirley worked as a nursery school teacher. She earned a Master's degree from Columbia University in early childhood education and quickly rose from being a preschool teacher to a consultant to the New York City Division of Day Care. She became an authority on child welfare and education and started to volunteer for political organisations - all of which were predominantly run by white men, particularly at the top. Shirley planned to change that.

She won a landslide victory for a seat in the New York State Assembly, and four years later won a seat in Congress running a grassroots campaign with the slogan, "Fighting Shirley Chisholm - Unbossed and Unbought."

She only appointed women to her staff, several of them African American women. "Fighting Shirley" got to work, and fight she did, demanding an appointment to a relevant committee for her constituency. She introduced more than 50 pieces of legislation and championed racial and gender equality, the plight of the poor, and ending the Vietnam War. She became the first Black woman, and second woman ever, to serve on the powerful House Rules Committee.

She ran for President in the 1972 election on a platform of change. She was proud to be both Black and a Woman, but said she ran as neither. She ran as a candidate who represented the people, and criticized the way government seemed to only represent the interests of older, white men. She faced discrimination, and had to file a lawsuit to be included in televised speeches and debates. Shirley was especially disappointed by the lack of support she received from Gloria Steinem and other prominent members of the Women's movement as well as from Black male political leadership. She campaigned wherever she was able and won 152 delegates in the primaries. She lost the nomination to George McGovern, but she saw her presidential bid as encouragement for greater participation in politics by minorities.

Shirley served seven terms in Congress before retiring and she went on to teach at Mount Holyoke College. She co-founded the National Political Congress of Black Women. Of her legacy, Chisholm said, "I want to be remembered as a woman ... who dared to be a catalyst of change." She paved the way for women in politics. She passed away in 2005, but her legacy lives on and her influence continues to inspire women today to run for office.

"We have to be visible. We should not be ashamed of who we are."

Sylvia Rivera

Who was Sylvia Rivera?

1951-2002

Sylvia Rivera was a queen before her time.

Born to a Puerto Rican father and Venezuelan mother in the Bronx, Sylvia was assigned male at birth and named Ray. Little Ray was orphaned by age three and adopted by her grandmother. Granny had little love for her effeminate grandson who liked to dress in girls clothes and wear makeup. Sylvia started hustling on the streets of Times Square when she was only 11, and soon left her grandmother's home forever. She was taken in by a community of drag queens, and Sylvia learned how to survive on the streets with their guidance. She spent the rest of her life in periods of homelessness, drug addiction, poverty, and in and out of prison.

Sylvia is rumored to have thrown one of the first bottles at police during the Stonewall uprising, when police raided the underground club looking for crossdressers. The crowd revolted that night which resulted in a week long rebellion across the city of New York. This uprising was really the beginning of the Gay Rights movement and it was all started by a few drag queens who were sick and tired of being unfairly persecuted by the police.

Sylvia joined the new Gay Activists Alliance and began working furiously to pass a Gay Rights bill in New York City. She was even arrested for climbing the walls of City Hall in a dress and high heels to crash a closed-door meeting on the bill. Yet, despite her heroic efforts, Transgender Rights were pushed aside by the increasingly mainstream Gay Rights movement, and her community remained on the margins. Her response was to do what she did best - fight back.
"Hell hath no fury like a drag queen scorned," Sylvia warned.

Her sassy attitude made her a legend in the LGBTQ+ community. Sylvia boldly inserted herself into the front lines of the movement, hijacking microphones to make speeches at events, and marching in the front of Pride Parades that had refused her participation. She organized against discrimination and injustice, finding allies in unlikely places.

Rivera saw herself in many of the trans street kids who ended up homeless and hustling, and felt compelled to help them. She started to call them "her children." Together with Marsha she founded STAR-Street Transvestite* Action Revolutionaries - a group dedicated to helping homeless young drag queens and trans Women of Color. When her dear friend Marsha's body was found floating in the Hudson River, Sylvia knew the cause of death was not suicide and pushed for an investigation. Soon she would attempt suicide herself, in that same river. She stepped away from activism for a time, but came back with a fury in the late 1990's.

Sylvia was fighting for the trans community even on her deathbed, but didn't live to see any of her dreams for her community realized. While the Gay Rights movement has made massive strides in the decades since her death, trans and gender non-conforming people are only now becoming visible within the movement, and winning Supreme Court cases. Sylvia has a street named after her in Greenwich Village, and her photograph is displayed at the National Portrait Gallery. Her greatest legacy is The Sylvia Rivera Law Project which provides legal assistance to transgender people regardless of income or race, and without facing harassment, discrimination or violence.

*at the time of the Stonewall riots, the gay community did not have the same extensive vocabulary to describe sexuality as we do today. Marsha and Sylvia were transgender women, but primarily referred to themselves as drag queens or transvestites, which have separate meanings today. Transvestite is now considered a derogatory term

Who was Wilma Rudolph?

1940-1994

Wilma was fast. She was the fastest woman on earth. But it didn't start that way.

Wilma was born prematurely to an African American family in Clarksville, Tennessee in the still segregated South. She was the 20th of 22 children, and was well loved and taken care of. She was sick for much of her childhood, surviving double pneumonia, scarlet fever, and whooping cough. A bout of polio left one leg crooked and her foot curved. Wilma spent a lot of time at home in her leg brace, dreaming. She couldn't go to a nearby hospital because it was reserved for white people only. Every week, between the ages of six and ten, she and her mother boarded a segregated bus and traveled 50 miles to a hospital where she could receive treatment. At home her mother and siblings massaged her leg multiple times a day. Then one day when she was nine years old, to the shock of her family and friends, she took off her brace and walked without it. It would take some time for her to move normally, but she was determined to run. As soon as she could she jumped right in to playing basketball with anyone she could find at the park, and then started track in high school. She loved running so much she would skip school to practice.

As a sophomore in high school, a well-known college women's track coach named Ed Temple noticed Wilma's talent at a basketball game and invited her to a summer training camp. Coach Temple was sure Wilma was good enough to compete in the Olympics. She was 16 and had never heard of the Olympics, but after some intense training, she made the team. She was the youngest person on the U.S. Olympic team. The people in her hometown worked together to raise money to buy Wilma the things she would need to travel to the 1956 Melbourne Games in style.

In the 200-meter event, she advanced to the semifinals but missed the cut for the finals. A crushing defeat. Her disappointment fired her up for the next event, the 4x100-meter relay. Wilma and her 3 teammates earned the Bronze medal. She vowed to return and do even better.

She came back home a hero and continued competing in basketball and track in high school. She earned a scholarship to Tennessee State and was looking forward to being the first in her family to attend college when she became pregnant. This might have meant the loss of her scholarship, but Coach Temple decided that if Wilma could manage being a mother, a student, and an athlete, he would break the rules and still offer her the scholarship. With the support of Wilma's family, it all worked out. After becoming a mother she noticed that she was even faster than before. She was slower with her starts, but would quickly catch up and outpace her competitors in dramatic finishes.

In competition leading up to the 1960 Olympics in Rome, she won the AAU nationals in the 200 meters, and set a new world record - 22.9 seconds. At the Games, the crowds chanted her name as she won Olympic Gold in every race she entered: the 100 meters, the 200 meters, and, with her 3 teammates the 4x100-meter relay, setting another world record. The crowd went wild! Wilma was the fastest woman in the world! She won nearly every event she competed in for the next few years.

Wilma used her victory to champion Women's and Civil Rights. She insisted she would only participate in an unsegregated homecoming parade in her hometown. It was the first integrated event in Clarkesville history. Wilma went on international goodwill tours and met ambassadors, famous entertainers, and President John F. Kennedy. Her story of overcoming brought her worldwide fame, and changed the way many white people in America thought about race and women in sports. She spoke out about gender parity in sports and the pay gap in athletics and in other fields. In the 1980s, she established the Wilma Rudolph Foundation to support young people in underserved communities through sports and academics.

In 1983, she was inducted into the U.S. Olympic Hall of Fame. Wilma was the first woman to win 3 Gold medals in Track and Field at a single Olympic games. Her notoriety brought unprecedented attention to women in the Olympics, especially to Women's Track and Field events. In 1994, at age 54, she died of brain cancer. She is survived by two daughters and two sons. Wilma inspired generations of women athletes, especially minority women athletes who faced so many barriers to achieving their dreams.

Draw yourself here:

Your Name:_____

How will you change
the world?

_____

_____

_____

_____

_____

_____

_____

_____

_____

_____

_____

_____

_____

_____

_____

_____

_____

_____

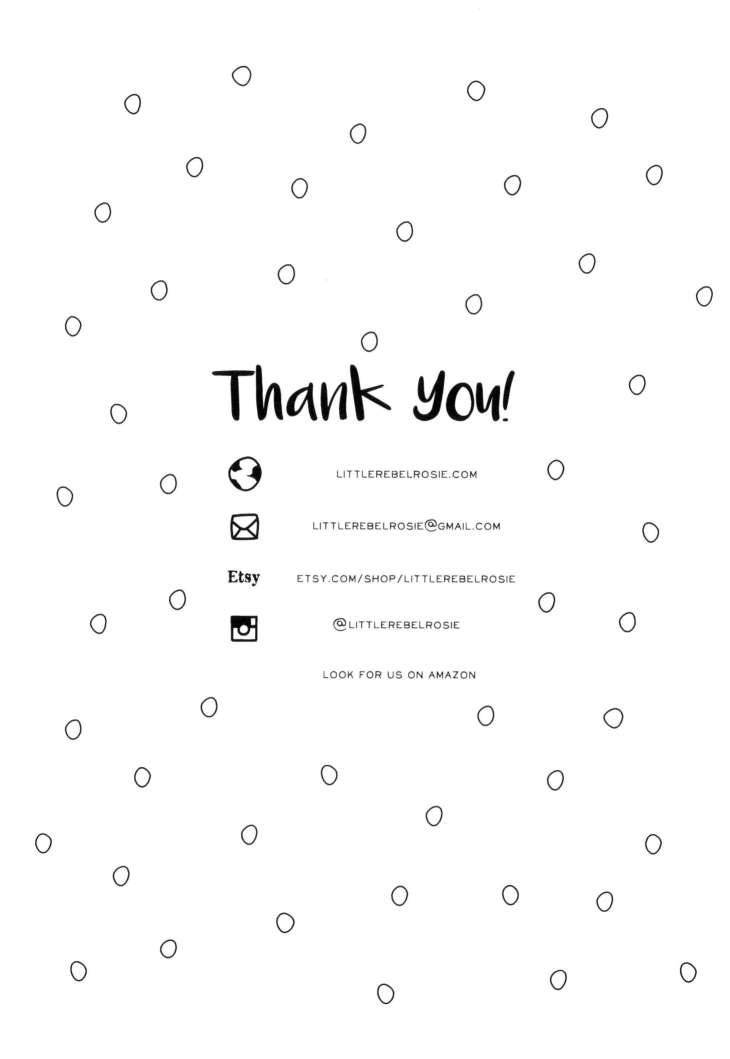

Thank you!

🌐 LITTLEREBELROSIE.COM

✉ LITTLEREBELROSIE@GMAIL.COM

Etsy ETSY.COM/SHOP/LITTLEREBELROSIE

📷 @LITTLEREBELROSIE

LOOK FOR US ON AMAZON

Made in the USA
Middletown, DE
07 December 2020